STEAM MEMORIES ON SHED : 1950's – 19

No. 98: SCOTTISH REGION E   DS

& THEIR MOTIVE POWER

62A to 62C & Sub Sheds

DAVID DUNN

Copyright Book Law Publications 2020

ISBN 978-1-913049-10-2

INTRODUCTION

In the number of main sheds located within the 62 group, this one had the smallest number of coded sheds of any in Scotland with just three: 62A Thornton, 62B Dundee Tay Bridge, and 62C Dunfermline. However, the number of sub sheds was quite impressive with no less than eight shared out amongst the three main sheds. At the heart of this group of sheds was the depot known as Thornton Junction, or simply Thornton and whose main business was to supply motive power to move coal from the Fife area collieries. Helping 62A to shift those millions of tons of coal a year was Dunfermline shed 62C, itself located in a strategic position in the coalfield. Dundee Tay Bridge shed 62B was not located within the coalfield and therefore its allocation reflected that fact. Whereas 62A and 62C had literally dozens of 0-6-0s and later 2-8-0s between them, 62B was more concerned with passenger, parcels and fish trains, its allocation featuring Pacifics, V2s, B1s, 4-4-0s, and because of the former cross-border inter action between the LNER and the LMS, Dundee had a number of ex-LMS Stanier Class 5s allocated at various times besides lesser types. The mix of classes handled by the main sheds, along with the handful of engines using the sub-sheds makes for an interesting pot-pourri of motive power seen by the cameras of enthusiasts during the final decades of steam in Scotland.

David Dunn, Cramlington, January 2020.

(*Cover*)   **See page 10.**

(*Previous Page*) **The western end of Dunfermline engine shed on 7th October 1950 with ex-works N15 No.69154 looking rather smart albeit a little dusty after its General overhaul at Cowlairs – 17th August to 2nd September – when it received a new boiler – No.2053 (reno.26478). A long-time resident of Dunfermline, the 0-6-2T was transferred away to Dundee on 15th August 1957. Just peeking out of the shed, sister No.69164, still in unlined black would have to wait until the following February before its next General overhaul and repaint. The shed roof seen here is the original built with the shed just before Grouping hence its rather tidy appearance.** *K.H. Cockerill (ARPT).*

Printed and bound by The Amadeus Press, Cleckheaton, West Yorkshire

First published in the United Kingdom by Book Law Publications, 382 Carlton Hill, Nottingham, NG4 1JA

THORNTON

A general view of Thornton Junction engine shed as it would have appeared on completion in 1933. Seen from its western end on 20th June 1959, the building was still in good condition but it was less than thirty years old. Consisting six stabling roads which projected through to the shed's east end, the layout included a two road repair shop on the south side which had a single pitched roof as opposed to the transverse multiple-pitched roofs straddling the running shed; one of the repair shop roads also projected into the east yard. In the distance can be seen the coaling plant which until about 1948 was certainly one of the highest structures in the area. One the north side of the shed lay four servicing roads where locomotive fires, ashpans and smokeboxes could be cleaned, engines watered and access to the mechanical coaler was gained. Along the north side of those roads were three sidings for full coal wagons used to feed the coaler; latterly a couple of those siding were used to store withdrawn locomotives or any requiring main works attention. On the left can be seen another siding taken over for storing 'laid-up' engines such as the D49 and D11 4-4-0s in view; note the state of the track on that latest siding! This shed replaced an establishment which dated from 1896 and which consisted four through roads but only had room for twenty under cover; the seventy-nine strong allocation of locomotives in 1927 certainly helped the authorities decide on creating a completely new depot. The 70ft turntable for the new depot was ordered from Cowans Sheldon in 1931 but although the LNER received some funding via the Government Loan Act for the relocation of the depot and new buildings, the shed itself was built from somewhat lightweight steel framing clad in corrugated iron sheets. *C.J.B. Sanderson (ARPT).* 3

The eastern end of Thornton junction shed during its final year as an operational steam shed. The date is 19th June 1966 and only one steam locomotive is in view – B1 No.61347 – with three of the depot's diesel shunters stabled on the left. The stabling shed roof was built in the style used by the North British Railway – and the Caledonian too – with elaborate smoke ventilators which had a touch of far-eastern charm about them. The B1 was a newcomer to Thornton having been transferred from 64A some eight weeks previously. This was to be its final shed and it was condemned on 4th April 1967 just as the shed was closed. One thing showing in this image but not in any other featured in this album is the mountain of colliery waste just discernible above and to the right of the diesels. It is some distance to the west of the depot and a few hundred feet high. Now you might wonder what the relevance of that tip was but the facts will become clearer as we proceed. On the right is Glenrothes Colliery – or just Rothes Colliery depending on your sources – which was a new production unit and the first new colliery created by the National Coal Board in Scotland. *A. Ives (ARPT).*

B1 No.61349 passing the water tower at Thornton during the summer of 1966. The rather neat, clean and tidy surroundings of the depot are worthy of comment; it was a time of massive transition from steam to diesel or more radically from operational to closed depots when nobody really bothered about anything. Thornton it seems was the exception. This is the east end of the depot on what appears to by a glorious morning in Fife. *David Dunn collection*.

Even in July 1958 clean seems to have been the order of the day; the wheelbarrow seemingly on its rounds collecting the odd mound of unauthorised rubbish after a summer shower. Resident D34s 62467 GLENFINNAN and 62468 GLEN ORCHY are in various states of mechanical condition with the former showing the subtle signs of a Heavy Intermediate at Inverurie 29th April to 26th May 1958 whilst its sister hadn't been near main works for eighteen months or so and would not be doing so ever again. No.62468 was condemned on 3rd September and by the end of October it was resident in the scrapyard at Inverurie its forty-six years of operation over! After its 'refresher' in May No.62467 kept going until 10th August 1960 when it too was condemned. They were both built at Cowlairs in September 1913 but both were cut up at Inverurie. *A.R. Thompson (ARPT).*

A peek into the future! Or more correctly an unknown date in 1968 with withdrawn Peppercorn A2 No.60532 awaiting entry into the Thornton repair shop. Formerly named BLUE PETER, this Pacific had been withdrawn from stock on 31st April 1966 at Aberdeen Ferryhill shed, the last of its class. Peppercorn's other Pacifics had all been scrapped by June 1966 and interest was aroused to preserve this particular engine. So, it was laid aside and on 21st August 1968 it was purchased for preservation but not just as an inert piece of metal. Part of the agreement in the sale was to have it in working condition. This visit may well have had some connection with the sale and its conditions? The rest of the story is now just history. However, Thornton hadn't quite finished as a motive power depot when it closed to steam in April 1967. There were a number of diesel shunters still active and they were maintained for a good few years until this final curtain was dropped on 62A in 1969 when the shed was demolished. Main line diesels had used the depot as a stabling point and even when the shed itself disappeared, dozens of locomotives could be found at weekends in the sidings. *David Dunn collection*.

J88 No.8337 is shed pilot on this Saturday – 26th June 1948 – and its crew do not spot photographer Ken Cockerill scanning the little 0-6-0T just before it blocked out the mining workings in the distance. This image has been included simply to show the temporary headgear in place over one of the shafts being sunk to create Rothes Colliery. The shaft was still open to the elements although a canopy has been erected around the upper section of the headgear in order to take some of the weather away from the workings. Shaft sinking started in 1946 and the headgear was a recent addition, albeit temporary, to enable men and equipment to be lowered now in cages to a substantial depth and then return the cages to the surface with spoil from the sinking and developing headings. A truly massive undertaking, the colliery towers which eventually came to dominate the local area, and become a navigational aid from the North Sea, were some years away yet from being erected. What of the J88? No.8337 became 68337 on 10th August 1951 and was condemned on 8th November 1955, being broken up at Cowlairs. It appears to have spent all of its life serving the two Thornton sheds having been placed into traffic in April 1909 as NBR No.238. *K.H. Cockerill (ARPT).*

The crew of J88 No.68335 pose for the photographer in July 1950. The 0-6-0T had not long since returned from a General overhaul at Cowlairs – 17th May to 3rd June 1950 – which would see it through to December 1956 when it required another boiler change. Having been allocated to Thornton for most of its life, the engine transferred away to Haymarket in December 1959 but ended its days at the former Caledonian shed at Dawsholm where it was condemned on 8th October 1962. *C.J.B. Sanderson (ARPT).*

K4 No.61996 LORD OF THE ISLES beneath the Thornton coaling plant on 22nd May 1961. The Gresley 2-6-0 had been allocated to 62A since 24th April 1959 having been transferred from Eastfield after twenty years plying the West Highland line to Fort William and Mallaig. Sisters 61993 LOCH LONG, 61994 THE GREAT MARQUESS, 61995 CAMERON OF LOCHEIL, and 61998 MACLEOD OF MACLEOD also came to Thornton in 1959. Thornton was to prove to be their final home; less than five months after this image was recorded No.61996 was condemned and then taken to Inverurie for breaking up. No.61998 followed but 61993 and 61995 were broken up at Townhill, Dunfermline and 61994 was of course preserved. *F.W. Hampson (ARPT).*

No.61994 in 1963 alongside the main line at Thornton; having been withdrawn in October 1961 in working order, the K4 was eventually moved from Thornton with Eastfield looking a likely destination according to the legend on the cylinder casing. Note the 62A shed plate still in situ! *W. Coulson (ARPT)*.

No.90468, one of Thornton's WD Austerity 2-8-0s stables on a repair road with an unidentified ex-NBR 0-6-0 on an unknown date but circa 1960s. 62A had been home to fifty-one of these robust and useful 8Fs, the first four arriving in December 1945 when the LNER purchased two hundred of them. Many spent their whole lives at Thornton and no less than twenty-one were condemned there. Our subject locomotive arrived on 19th August 1963 and was condemned on 22nd April 1967, the last of Thornton's 2-8-0s and the only one which worked until closure. Note the BR Standard top-feed which replaced the original top-feed on this engine in April 1959. Most of the Scottish Region WD 2-8-0s were fitted with the BR Standard top feed whereas all the other regions – except the WR who provided their fleet with the GWR style top-feed – kept the examples provided with the engines from building. *A. Dodgson (ARPT).*

The photographer's subject here in 1966 is the so-called 'light-tunnel' which was a wartime building provided so that locomotives could be repaired in black-out conditions. Basically light-tight, the structure was sealed so as not to emit any light which might have given German bombers a guide or clue as to a possible target. The 'tunnel' was kept for further use after the ending of hostilities and remained as part of the repair assets until closure of the shed to steam. *J.W. Armstrong (ARPT)*.

D30 No.62429 THE ABBOT in the east yard at Thornton shed on the last day of February 1953. Still looking half decent from a General overhaul received at Cowlairs in the previous September, the 4-4-0 was some four and a half years away from withdrawal with a couple more works visits planned beforehand – admitted light repairs – prior to being packed off to the works at Inverurie in September 1957 for scrapping. Thornton became the last stronghold of the ex-NBR 4-4-0s and a visit on Wednesday 6th May 1959 D34 62492 GLEN GARVIN was station pilot, with 62475 GLEN BEASDALE having been employed on the same duties during the last week of April. Apparently the regular pilot, an ex-CR 0-4-4T No.55217, was otherwise not available! Other Thornton 4-4-0s, 62418 THE PIRATE and 62478 GLEN QUOICH were on passenger trains. All four would be gone by the end of the year with two condemned in June, one in August and 62478 on 15th December. *C.J.B. Sanderson (ARPT)*.

St Margaret's D30 'Scott' No.62421 LAIRD O'MONKBARNS stabled alongside the north wall of Thornton shed in July 1958. Already forty-four years old, the 4-4-0 had finished with main works visits some three years previously and was now relying on shed fitters to keep her going. They must have done a good job in Edinburgh because this D30 and sister No.62426 CUDDIE HEADRIGG of Stirling were the last two of their class to go. The pair were condemned on 25th June 1960 and both ended up from whence they came. *A.R. Thompson (ARPT)*.

The days of the D11/2 in Scotland were all but over by 2nd April 1961. Truth be known they had been made redundant a few years beforehand but various seasonal requirements saw some of them activated now and again. This line-up at Thornton includes Nos.62686 THE FIERY CROSS and 62687 LORD JAMES OF DOUGLAS both of which were allocated to Eastfield but had been farmed out to Thornton for storage. The pair of them were soon condemned 62686 on 27th July and 62687 on 2nd August. They were taken to Cowlairs and Inverurie respectively for cutting up. These two D11/2s were stored at Arbroath in 1956 with others of their ilk – see later – and again at Dundee in 1959. *N.W. Skinner (ARPT).*

J37 No.64570 has received half of a paint job on the smokebox door probably to cover scorching. The date of this image is 22nd September 1965 and we see the 0-6-0 at home awaiting its next duty. The J37 transferred to 62A on 20th October 1964 from Grangemouth and Thornton was to prove to be its last home with withdrawal taking place on 19th November 1966. It was purchased by a scrapyard in Airdrie on 9th February 1967. *N.W. Skinner (ARPT)*.

THE PIRATE laid-up on 22nd June 1959 before being condemned on 6th August. Would the tender be emptied of that pile of coal – 7-tons – or would the private scrap merchant who purchased the locomotive during the following October be happy to receive such an abundance of heating materials? In the background Rothes Colliery is now in production with waste being sent to the tip located at the western end of Thornton's shed yard besides the waste from the development period their was five years of waste during the further development driving roads and creating faces. One of the self-tipping cable cars can be seen about to cross over the main line on its journey to the tip. *F.W. Hampson (ARPT).*

It is late-August 1965 and J38 No.65920 has just returned to Thornton Junction shed from a Heavy Intermediate overhaul at Inverurie, which was to be its final shopping. The 0-6-0 transferred into Thornton from Dalry Road on 7th March 1965 and was only on the premises for nine weeks when it was called to Inverurie. Although No.65920 received this major overhaul so late in the great scheme, it appears not to have made much difference as it was condemned on 19th November 1966 and then sold on to the Arnott Young scrapyard in Old Kirkpatrick. *F. Coulton*.

Alongside No.65920 during that early afternoon in August 1965 was an unusual visitor for this mainly freight shed. St Margarets A3 No.60052 PRINCE PALATINE had accompanied the J38 back from Aberdeenshire after it too had visited the works at Inverurie, albeit only for minor repairs. The Pacific would return to Edinburgh within a few days unless 62A found some work for it. This A3 was to become the last of the class and after being condemned on 17th January 1966 it languished at St Margarets until the following June when it was sold for scrap. No.60041 was also waiting at 64A for the scrap man after being condemned in December but its purchase did not take place until September. *F. Coulton*.

Inside the Thornton repair shop in late August 1965 with Dunfermline based J38 No.65934 receiving some attention to its running gear. The 0-6-0 survived the ordeal and went back into traffic soon afterwards. The last of the class to be built in 1926, No.65934 was condemned on the last day of 1966. *F. Coulton.*

WD No.90596 was a latecomer to 62A, arriving from Aberdeen Ferryhill on 23rd April 1966 and remaining until condemned on 4th April the following year. This undated north-easterly facing image of the 2-8-0 beneath the coaling plant was therefore recorded within those dates. *F. Coulton*.

Another view of the coaler this time seen from a south-easterly direction with J37 No.64570 taking water and B1 No.61103 about to. The Thompson 4-6-0 spent all of its short twenty year life working from Thornton junction shed, its demise on 14th July 1966 saw it sold to a scrapyard in Airdrie. The 0-6-0 transferred from Grangemouth to Thornton on 20th October 1964. It was its final shed and was condemned 19th November 1966. It too went on a one-way trip to Airdrie. *F. Coulton*.

J88 No.68353 stabled outside the shed on 25th August 1956. A relative newcomer to Thornton, the 0-6-0T arrived from Kittybrewster on 12th December 1943. It was to remain at 62A until condemned on 12th February 1962 one of the last although No.68345 at Kipps was the last of them being condemned 29th December 1962. Up to 1955 Thornton shed usually had around eight of these useful tank engines allocated but during that year the first withdrawals took place and from there onwards the decline set in at 62A. Note the Thornton legend on the bufferbeam and the unknown SA marking on the smokebox door behind the handles. Meanwhile over at the colliery we can just get a look inside one of the new concrete and glass towers protecting the winding mechanism. As yet the development headgear is still in place – its steelwork being visible – as is the temporary winding house, the roof of which is just visible outside the tower. Much work has yet to be done on the surface including erecting the Koepe electric winding gear within the concrete towers. History was being created on the other side of the main railway line. *C.J.B. Sanderson (ARPT).*

J72 No.69012 was transferred from Ipswich to Thornton Junction with sister 69013 on 3rd February 1952. When they actually reached the Kingdom of Fife is unknown but 69012 decided to stay at 62A until condemned nine years later. No.69013 meantime moved on to St Margarets on 17th December 1957 but on 25th August 1956 Cecil Sanderson managed to capture the six-coupled tank on film inside the western end of the main shed just three months after the tank received a 'General' at Inverurie. That repair was the only major overhaul administered during the J72's short twelve-year life. However, the 0-6-0T certainly got around compared with 69012: Built at Darlington as their works number 2094, she was put into traffic on 28th December 1949 and sent to Doncaster shed. Five months later on 28th May 1950 she was transferred – with 69012 – from 36A to Ipswich. We then know that the pair then left 32B for 62A on what by any standards was a marathon journey. After just over three years at 64A, 69013 went to Polmadie on 1st March 1961 which was something of a first with an ex-LNER (NER) design tank engine taking up residence in the former Caley-LMS stronghold (if the transfer had taken place a month later eyebrows would not have been raised as far). Three months later the J72 was sent to Motherwell where it was accepted gracefully as sister 69015 had preceded it to 66B by four months, courtesy of Parkhead shed. Neither J72 lasted long at Motherwell; 69015 withdrawn on 14th September 1961 and was sent to Heatheryknowe for breaking up two months later. Our subject engine lasted until 22nd January 1962 and was later sold to a private scrapyard. *C.J.B. Sanderson (ARPT)*.

D49 No.62712 MORAYSHIRE spent the whole of its life working in what was known as the LNER Scottish Area; its initial shed being Dundee. It spent the greater part of its thirty-three years at Perth shed where from August 1930 to 4th March 1944 it plied the main line between Perth and Edinburgh hauling amongst other expresses the Perth section of the Anglo-Scottish express passenger train THE FLYING SCOTSMAN. The 4-4-0 came to Thornton on 27th January 1958 after nearly fourteen years in Edinburgh where it did stints at both Haymarket and St Margaret's sheds. This image of the rather grimy engine was captured on 20th June 1959 almost two years after it had received its final General overhaul and repaint. Although we can't see the right side BR crest on the tender, No.62712 carried one of the wrong-facing examples applied in August 1957 at Darlington works. Although Thornton was gaining a reputation as a stronghold for Scottish Region 4-4-0s at this time, this D49 did not stay to the end and was transferred away to Hawick on 4th April 1960. Condemned on 3rd July 1961, No.62712 then did a spell on stationary boiler duties at Slateford laundry but was sold into preservation on 6th January 1965. *C.J.B. Sanderson (ARPT)*.

Another of the active D49s at Thornton in June 1959 was No.62728 CHESHIRE – of the seven allocated during that summer at least half were stored – which had also served the whole of its life at Scottish sheds. 62A proved to be its last home having transferred from Dundee on 21st February 1957. Like sister 62712, this D49 was also given a BR crest with a wrong-facing lion on the right side. Facing forward, the lion and wheel should have been facing left; it was never corrected. No.62728 went to Darlington works on 29th October next and never came out being condemned on that very day! *C.J.B. Sanderson (ARPT)*.

J36 No.65345 stabled on the north side of the shed on 20th June 1959 with an unidentified WD 2-8-0. By this date the remaining J36 were getting long-in-the-tooth and this particular engine's existence was looking far from.....! In actuality the 0-6-0 had another eight years of work in front of it, all, except for a year at Bathgate – December '65 to December '66 – before retiring at Thornton on 5th June 1967. In 1959 just three J36 worked from 62A; other sheds had more, 61C had five, 62B four, 62C six, 64A six, 64E seven, 64F fifteen, 64G four, 65E ten, even Polmadie had a pair! Besides these sheds many former LNER establishments had one, two or three of the J36, a fact which reflects even then when many of the engines were past or approaching their sixtieth year just how useful they still were. At Grouping Thornton shed had sixteen of the class allocated and that number remained constant up to 1933 when the new six-road shed opened. It is interesting to note that at Nationalisation just three of the class remained at Thornton – 5218, 5291, and 5345 – and although two of them had gone by 1965, our subject engine was still 'on the books' as it had been at 31st December 1922 and for many years before hand too! *C.J.B. Sanderson (ARPT)*.

We have to show one of the few BR Standards which worked from Thornton Junction. This is Class 4 2-6-0 No.76109 which together with 76110 and 76111 were sent new to 62A from Doncaster works in August 1957. After a couple of years they moved on to Dunfermline in 1960 from where two of them worked until the end of 1966. At Thornton they worked the passenger services to Edinburgh and Glasgow once entrusted to the D11/2s which were now stored on a permanent basis. The date of this image is 20th June 1959 and the Cl.4 is carrying the usual coating of grime associated with the period. The white blobs decorating the smokebox are apparently from a painting prank gone wrong rather than something feathery with a beak relieving itself from the roof rafters. *C.J.B. Sanderson (ARPT)*.

WD No.90117, in ex-works condition at the west end of the shed 20th June 1959: The 2-8-0 had just returned from a Heavy Intermediate overhaul at Cowlairs – 19th May to 11th June 1959. No.90117 would have another H/I in 1961 however, besides that event the locomotive would also receive two Heavy Generals – in 1960 and 1963 – and still be outlived by the J36 highlighted on page 28. Transferring to Thornton from Dunfermline on 2nd December 1956, No.90117 was condemned at Thornton 20th January 1967 almost six months before No.65345. Incidentally the two locomotives were built at different factories in Glasgow just a few miles apart, the WD at the North British Locomotive Co. works in March 1943 whilst the J36 came out of the North British Railway works at Cowlairs in December 1900. *C.J.B. Sanderson (ARPT)*.

The splendour of Glenrothes (also listed as Rothes) Colliery on 11th June 1962 with its two huge winding towers! Sinking of this coal mine started in 1946 and on the strength of its projected annual production of saleable coal – more than 1.6 million tons – British Railways decided to create a new marshalling yard at Thornton Junction to supersede the old yard and a number of smaller yards in the area. Building work on the yard proceeded so that the opening coincided with the opening of the new colliery nearby. One must remember that coal in the 1950s was deemed to be the fuel of the future in the United Kingdom and other countries too. On 1st January 1955 progress was being made on the new marshalling yard which occupied sixty-five acres with an estimated cost of £1,350,000. Full operation of Thornton's new yard came into effect from Monday 26th November 1956. The yard operated very successfully but was never to reach its full potential because of the problems at the adjacent colliery. However, by the summer of 1957 when the colliery was expected to start full production three 350 h.p. 0-6-0DE shunting locomotives were employed thus: hump pilot; and two east end pilots. A visit on 27th June that year found the trio employed were 13275, 13337, and 13340 part of the 62A fleet which had six of the BR built 0-6-0DEs at that time. Representing steam was a J36 0-6-0 which was engaged as an assisting engine. The Fife coalfield was by 1957 the most productive in Scotland with more than 24,000 miners employed. Thornton yard was going to be in the centre of the coalfield handling the production of about thirty mines. The NCB meanwhile got on with their new 'super pit' and by 1957 the massive concrete clad winding towers enclosing the latest Koepe electric winders were completed whilst below ground the initial coal faces had been developed ready for full scale production. The winders lifted conventional cages with minecars – the skip hoists used in later mine developments were still being finely tuned – which were ejected onto a minecar circuit at the pithead. The mine was opened by HM Queen Elizabeth II on 30th June 1958 – she even descended, suitably attired, to the coal face where the ceremony took place – and the Minister for Scotland stated that Rothes pit had a lifespan of 100 years! A new town – Glenrothes – was built to serve the miners and their families. However, although 1960 was its peak year of production with some 1,235 personnel engaged, only 139,000 tons of saleable coal reached the surface in 1961. Below ground geological problems started to manifest themselves and then the flooding started in earnest. The latter proved to be the undoing of the pit and in 1962 production was halted and it was decided to close the mine. In 1969 it was abandoned completely but the towers remained until blown-up in March 1993, an event which symbolised the end of the NCB. The projected cost of building and developing the colliery was £1.65 million but in reality it cost some £20 million. It became a huge political embarrassment with only five years of production and then only in part because the flooding had started during development. The records associated with the mine were placed in the Public Record Office, closed and deemed inaccessible until 2000! *Howard Forster*.

ANSTRUTHER

Over to the coast now at Anstruther on Tuesday 21st August 1956 and we find J35 No.64521 moving off the shed. This sub-shed of Thornton Junction dated from 1883 and had replaced an older shed belonging to the Levens & East Fife Railway which was taken over by the North British Railway in 1877. From this angle the shed yard matches the condition of the closed and derelict passenger platform of the first station but the shed was certainly operational until 1960; the passenger station which was open was out of frame to the left and was operational until September 1965. At this time in the mid-'50s a D30 or D34 would stable overnight in the shed with a J35 for company, the 4-4-0 taking care of the first passenger train on the Crail-Edinburgh (Waverley) service whilst the 0-6-0 would work the pick-up. Evidence of the goods yard can be seen on the right with new building taking place? *C.J.B. Sanderson (ARPT).*

Anstruther on 1st August 1966 with closure complete and dereliction and decay working in unison trying to return the facilities back to nature. The shed roof vents have started their inevitable lean outwards and would probably hit the ground long before a demolition crew would arrive to tidy the place up. Note that one of the shed roads has been lifted already whilst a lot of goods vehicles remain clustered around the contracting facilities. The shed was closed in December 1960 and amongst the locomotives stabling overnight in those final years was one of the trio of Thornton Cl.4 Standard 2-6-0s which had lost some of their passenger work to diesel units. *C.J.B. Sanderson (ARPT).*

BURNTISLAND

Steady Decline! This is Burntisland engine shed and works on 13th April 1957. A large conical-roofed roundhouse used to stand behind the facade and water tower, the arch of which doubled as shelter for the resident motive power which on this day is an unidentified J83. Before Thornton shed relocated to a larger site in 1933, Burntisland used to have a fairly large allocation compared to its BR status of sub-shed to Thornton with just two or three 0-6-0 tender engines and a couple of 0-6-0 tank engines as residents. Indeed the allocation on the last day of the North British Railway's existence was more than the sheds at Aberdeen (19), Berwick (25), Hawick (20), Perth (23), and Stirling (25), and was as follows: D51 – 1471; E7 – 1249; J31 – 1122, 1188; J33 – 21, 148, 178; J34 – 30, 163, 529, 533, 541, 551, 561, 1420, 1474; J36 – 616, 643, 677, 682, 762, 794; J88 – 117, 119, 836, 837, 839; N15 – 61, 65, 914. Total 30. Five years later on 31st December 1927 ten engines had gone but some, now with LNER numbers, had remained thus: J36 – 9248, 9616, 9643, 9644, 9662, 9677, 9681, 9682, 9708, 9762, 9794; J88 – 9117, 9119, 9836, 9837, 9839; N15 – 9065, 9174, 9225; Y9 – 10086. Total 20. By 31st December 1932 further changes had occurred and reductions continued: J36 – 9248, 0357, 9643, 9677, 9681, 9682, 9708, 9762, 9794; J69 – 7358, 7379; J88 – 9117, 9836, 9837. Total 14! And so the decline carried on. Twenty years later in February 1952 Burntisland housed – one J35, two J37, and two J83. Four years on to 18th March 1956 and these four resided: 64565, 65921, 68453, and 68459. By the summer of 1966 one diesel shunter – D2580 became the last of the line. The 'stable' had been closed in officially 1958 but in 1966 the place was demolished! *C.J.B. Sanderson (ARPT).*

The facade of the old roundhouse with the former locomotive works in the background on a dull Saturday 26th June 1948. A J83 – 68451, 68453, 68456, 68458, 68459, 68465, 68467; it could have been any one of these seven examples which were all allocated to Thornton Junction at that time and came to Burntisland in pairs on a weekly rota. The erstwhile roundhouse, which was an actual round shed with a high conical roof, had opened in 1847, the locomotive headquarters of the Edinburgh & Northern Railway. Never having visited the building, this writer cannot qualify if the windows set into this building were part of a faux facade or were those spaces above the arch utilised as offices perhaps? *K.H. Cockerill (ARPT).*

The site on 21st August 1966 with clearance of the old shed and works site proceeding slowly. Yes another British summer, damp and dull with rain threatening! Inside the archway is Hunslet 0-6-0 diesel shunter D2580 which was itself not long for this world – having arrived at Thornton from the makers just before Christmas 1958, the 0-6-0DM would work from 62A until 8th June 1968. D2580 was purchased by BR for use at Thornton, ten such diesels D2576–D2585 going new to the depot between July 1958 and April 1959. Although a couple were withdrawn in 1967, the bulk of them were withdrawn en masse on 8th June 1968. The reasons for the withdrawal; there were a few actually: They were non-standard; they didn't have much in the way of suitable work anymore; they were purchased at a time when shunting jobs were contracting at a rapid rate and with hindsight should never have been bought but British jobs were at stake and politics is always in the mix somewhere. They were good machines but! A few years earlier on 9th August 1959 two of the Hunslet diesels were resident here – D2576 and D2583. The complete withdrawal of motive power from this site took forty-three years to achieve but shortly after this image was recorded in late August 1966 the exercise was completed. *J.W. Armstrong (ARPT).*

(*opposite, top*) Methil docks in the distance seen in September 1968 from the site of the erstwhile Wellesley Colliery which was located just south-wet of the dock. Although the BR stabling point is somewhat difficult to pinpoint from here, the image gives a fair idea of the railway layout in the area which was also part of the Wemyss Private Railway. Indeed, as can be seen, steam still ruled on the colliery lines. As an aside, anyone contemplating building an industrial railway based on this site or even a freelance layout might spend some time studying this image for pointers; its full of 'anything goes!' *Ken Groundwater (ARPT). (opposite)* The stabling point located on a siding at the western end of Methil docks. On 22nd August 1953 three of the residents included J88 No.68322, and N15s Nos.69223, and 69150. The J88 was double-shifted and was designated Leven Dock No.1 Pilot. On 10th October 1952 J88 No.68322 was Pilot whilst N15s Nos.69211, 69223 and 69224 were shunting and tripping around the dock. On 18th March 1956 the stabling point contained N15s Nos.69013, 69143, 69153, and 69224. Modernisation reached the docks not long after Thornton started to receive its quota of diesel shunters on the allocation and Methil saw two 350 h.p. 0-6-0DE in use with two 200 h.p. 0-6-0DMs alongside. On 9th August 1959 the stabling point produced D2578, D2584, D3339, and D3340. Note the coal tipping gantries in the background. *C.J.B. Sanderson (ARPT).*

LADYBANK

Ladybank shed on Sunday 25th August 1957 with one steam locomotive hiding inside the shed whilst a Matisa track maintenance machine stables out of the way alongside the coaling stage. When British Railways took over the running of the UK railway system it inherited numerous small engine sheds such as this along with all the large sheds which used to dole out the motive power to establishments like Ladybank on a varying timescale basis. For instance Ladybank took in from Thornton two J35s, two J36, one J37, and a J69 'tar tank' as they were known in Fife. A visit on Sunday 18th March 1956 found the following at home and probably one of the largest gatherings before run-down of the shed towards its closure in 1958: J35 Nos.64464, 64466, 64477, J37 No.64635, N15 No.69211. A visit in September 1961 found a solitary diesel shunter: Hunslet 204 h.p. 0-6-0DM D2581. There was no mention of track machinery. *C.J.B. Sanderson (ARPT)*.

62B DUNDEE (Tay Bridge)

The western end of Dundee Tay Bridge shed, showing all six roads on Wednesday 17th August 1966. Thompson B1 No.61180, Gresley V2 No.60813, and Peppercorn A2 No.60530 SAYAJIRAO await their next jobs. *Trevor Ermel.*

The coaling plant at Dundee Tay Bridge shed with a V2 approaching from the west and a J37 seemingly replenished and making its way back to the shed which was located behind the cameraman's right shoulder. The roof of Dundee West shed, the former Caledonian establishment, can be seen above the V2; the date, 1st May 1965. *John Boyes (ARPT).*

An unknown date in 1963 finds two Pacifics – Nos.60528 TUDOR MINSTREL and 60532 BLUE PETER – looking exceedingly filthy in the shed yard. Both of these engines transferred from Aberdeen Ferryhill to Tay Bridge shed on 19th June 1961. The former returned to 61B on 24th April 1966, whilst the latter finally returned north on 4th December 1966. *I.W. Coulson (ARPT)*.

Dundee shed from across the main line showing the NBR period construction with the transverse multiple pitched roofs; this building was erected in 1878 and was something of a standard design not only with the NBR but also it appears that the Caledonian railway also adopted a similar outline. It is 22nd August 1966 now and A2 No.60530 is still hogging the western end yard. *J.W. Armstrong (ARPT).*

TUDOR MINSTREL in 1963; again we have no date but it appears that this image was captured after the last-but-one photograph showing the engine in that disgraceful external condition. This looks like a 'shed clean' rather than a works job and besides the Pacific hadn't been in shops since a visit to Doncaster in July 1962, and it was not due in again until February 1965 when Darlington carried out a Casual Light repair. *I.W. Coulson (ARPT).*

C16 No.67486 spent the greater part of its life working from Dundee Tay Bridge shed and in this 24th May 1949 image, captured when the Atlantic tank was just west of the coaling plant, the combination of BRITISH RAILWAYS insignia with lining shows up well and was to become fairly common amongst this class with no less than ten of them receiving such between 23rd September 1948 and 28th May 1949. After fifteen years in Glasgow, the C16 had transferred from Eastfield to Dundee on 30th May 1931 and was to remain at the shed for the next twenty-nine years. Note that as yet the engine is not wearing a shed plate, the 62B batch probably not yet cast. *K.H. Cockerill (ARPT)*.

Resident Stanier Cl.5 No.44722 soaks in the last rays of the evening sun in September 1966 on its way to the water column outside the north-eastern end of the shed. This end of the running shed was built with four roads whereas the south-western end has six roads. At some time after the LNER took over the depot, a repair shop was built over the two roads at the south-east corner. No.44722 was amongst a batch of five Cl.5s which were transferred into 62B during 1966: 44720 August 1966 ex-Perth, withdrawn October 1965; 44722 April 1966 ex-Perth, back to 63A November 1966; 44879 April 1966 ex-Perth, return 63A November 1966; 45127 August 1966 ex St Margarets, withdrawn November 1966; 45473 April 1966 ex-Perth, withdrawn November 1966. They weren't the only Cl.5s to have been allocated to Tay Bridge shed because 44954 arrived from Carstairs in September 1949 and remained at 62B until April 1960 when Carstairs beckoned it back. Then in September 1951 two others arrived thus: No.45330 ex-Dunfermline then to Kingmoor in July 1952; No.45384 ex-Shrewsbury, and to Corkerhill in April 1960; in October 1954 No.45486 transferred from Polmadie and then left in April 1960 also to 67A. Finally, in February 1955 No.45164 was transferred from Perth; it too went to Corkerhill in April 1960. *J.W. Armstrong (ARPT).*

Being made ready for the road on 6th July 1965, J37 No.64597 is oiled by its driver whilst in the cab the fireman tends the fire so that by the time the 0-6-0 gets to its first job the boiler will be ready for hard work. Alongside sister No.64608, another Tay Bridge resident, is beginning to lose its cabside numbers; its last repaint was some five years in the past. *A.R. Thompson (ARPT).*

Resident D34 No.62485 GLEN MURRAN outside the BR-built repair shop extension in July 1958. The 4-4-0 was about to begin its final year allocated to Tay Bridge prior to transfer to Dunfermline on 17th August 1959. It was condemned at 62C on 29th March 1960 and taken to Inverurie for scrap. The D34 had transferred to Dundee from Thornton in December 1945, and was the only member of her class to grace the 62B books throughout the BR period. Strangely, at Grouping D34 No.505 GLEN CONA was another singleton of the class which was allocated to Tay Bridge shed but in August 1931 it moved away to Thornton. *A.R. Thompson (ARPT)*.

Now here is an interesting image: Two B1s are prepared for work and are captured on film inside the shed giving the roof members a good coating of pollutants, corrosive gases, and goodness knows what in the absence of any smoke ventilators. The date is 6th July 1965 and by now authority was aware that any money spent repairing engine shed roofs, or indeed any section of the premises was money wasted. Tay Bridge shed like most of the former steam locomotive sheds was in line for demolition once steam had gone and so why bother. Nos.61147 and 61403 were both 62B residents and would remain so to their withdrawal. Worthy of note the smokebox doors, position of number plates, lamp brackets, footstep and SC shed plates!! *A.R. Thompson (ARPT)*.

Now the D30s and D33s were not so rare at Dundee. This is 62438 PETER POUNDTEXT on 7th August 1957 working out its final couple of months prior to being condemned. This 4-4-0 transferred from Eastfield to Tay Bridge on 17th April 1943 with FATHER AMBROSE. They had been preceded by KETTLEDRUMMLE and LORD GLENVARLOCH during the pre-war years. Indeed THE ABBOT, JINGLING GEORDIE, and KENILWORTH had basically started their careers at Dundee as had THE TALISMAN. DUMBIEDYKES was one of the BR period transfers but it was gone by October 1953. During WW2 in May 1943 THE PIRATE came for six weeks then departed to Stirling for the briefest of residences there then returned to Dundee for a seven year stint. And so that was a resume of the D30s and their comings and goings at Dundee. 62438 was one of those cut up at Kilmarnock. I wonder what happened to those wonderful hand painted names on the splashers. D33 class: It turns out that only two of them regarded Tay Bridge shed as home and none of the class was named anyway! *F.W. Hampson (ARPT)*.

I fear the worse! No.62485 on 17ᵗʰ May 1959. But Thornton shed called as a sort of reprieve in August. *F.W. Hampson (ARPT)*.

A morning view of Tay Bridge engine shed in 1967, after the 1st May closure. The building is full of wagons and dead locomotives were tied-up with string for all sorts of reasons. Forty-five years previously on the last day of the North British Railway, 31st December 1922, the allocation was nothing if not varied with 78 locomotives 'on the books' contained within twenty-one classes: C10 – 902; C11 – 509, 868, 869; D25 – 598; D26 – 322, 327; D29 – 245, 359, 362, 896; D30 – 419, 420, 421, 422, 425; D31 – 765; D32 – 885, 886; D33 – 382, 866; D34 – 505; D50 – 1391; D51 – 1406, 1465; G8 – 1320, 1325, 1334, 1338; G9 – 349, 350, 351, 352, 355; J34 – 543, 553; J35 – 58, 194, 195, 197, 198, 207, 208, 228, 254, 335, 337, 364, 370, 376; J36 – 179, 609, 617, 618, 649, 675, 751, 774, 776, 778; J37 – 110, 111, 296, 315, 430, 431, 477, 479, 489, 517; J83 – 805, 808, 815, 819; J88 – 87; Y9 – 1084, 1092, 1098. *C.J.B. Sanderson (ARPT).*

The other end of the shed on that same morning; the silence must have been deafening, the melancholy overwhelming. It is not too hard to envisage a crowded shed once again with noise, smells, motion and a host of other things to assault your senses. Twenty five years after Grouping came Nationalisation and on the eve of that event the LNER had 75 locomotives allocated to Tay Bridge, a number similar to 1922 but the locomotives were of a somewhat different bunch but nevertheless some sixteen classes were involved thus: B1 – 1101, 1102, 1263; C15 – 7461, 7471, C16 – 7483, 7484, 7486, 7489, 7490, 7491, 7498, 7499; D29 – 2409, 2410, 2412; D30 – 2418, 2434, 2438; D34 – 2485; D49 – 2713, 2718, 2728; J24 – 5614, 5622; J35 – 4482, 4485, 4493, 4506, 4512, 4523, 4530; J36 – 5319, 5328, 5330, 5333, J37 – 4537, 4548, 4575, 4587, 4593, 4615, 4619, 4620, 4627, 4631, 4634; J39 – 4786, 4790, 4792, 4822, 4950; J83 – 8446, 8452, 8455, 8466; V2 – 804, 838, 840, 844, 920, 937, 969, 971; WD – 3071, 3077, 3123, 3142, 3194; Y9 – 8100, 8107, 8108, 8110, 8114, 8123; *C.J.B.Sanderson (ARPT).*

At Dundee West Mineral yard on 17th May 1959 some twenty-two locomotives were in store thus, in numerical order: **62426, 62470, 62484, 62485, 62674, 62684, 62686, 62687, 64530, 65309, 65330, 65930, 67484, 67486, 67490, 67491, 67496, 67501, 67502, 68535, 69136, 69164, and 69204.** *F.W. Hampson (ARPT)*.

ARBROATH

Arbroath engine shed on 23rd June 1957 under a rather moody sky which was not at all seasonal. Opened as a Joint affair – with the Caledonian and North British railways unusually collaborating – in 1897 to create this three-road, transverse pitched roof shed. Located on the Down side of the main line, the depot was just to the north of Arbroath station. A turntable was located behind the photographer. The fortunes of this shed waxed and waned with a seemingly lunar frequency and in this view the place looks abandoned and ready for demolition but inside, and hidden by the closed doors were four D11/2s which had taken up residency in early March 1956 and had come from Eastfield: Nos.62673, 62680, 62686, and 62689. The storage of the D11/2 class had started in 1953 as BR Standard classes and later diesel multiple units had taken over most of their work but this was the first time Arbroath had housed any of them. Prior to January 1956 four other engines were stored at Arbroath with ex-Caley 0-4-4Ts Nos.55173 – which went to Aviemore; 55217 – to Thornton Jct.; 55227 and C16 No.67486 went back to Dundee. Arbroath's allocation of operational engines on 15th March 1956 consisted of Ivatt Cl.2s Nos.46463, 46464 and C16 No.67484 all from Dundee; the Ivatt Cl.2s had arrived in 1952. Arbroath engine shed closed officially in 1959. Note the house on the hill to the right; all that is missing is a large tunnel mouth. *C.J.B. Sanderson (ARPT).*

C16 No.67491 in store inside Dundee West shed on 25th August 1957. A visit on Friday 19th October 1956 found nineteen engines inside the former LMS shed thus: 42691, 45486, 55227, 60804, 60844, 60969, 60971, 61180, 62434, 64530, 64613, 64620, 65907, 67484, 68123, 68551, 90198, 90463, and 90515. Some were simply stabled, others stored, whilst some were under repair. The fifty years old 70ft diameter outside turntable was still in use. *C.J.B. Sanderson (ARPT).*

Seasonal storage or a repair annexe for Tay Bridge shed? This is the inside of the ex-LMS shed on 20th April 1953 with D30 No.62427 DUMBIEDYKES sharing a road with a V2 and a WD 2-8-0. Note how clean and clear the air is inside the building indicating that locomotives in steam were not allowed inside! In the late 1950s this shed was refurbished to house and maintain diesel shunting locomotives and multiple units. On Sunday 3rd September 1961 the following diesels were stabled with not a steam locomotive in sight: 225 h.p. 0-4-0DH shunters 11709, 11710, D2711, 11712, D2714, 11715, 11716, and 350 h.p. 0-6-0DE shunter D3347. *C.J.B. Sanderson (ARPT)*.

A broadside of the N15 featured on the title page. Doesn't she look grand? The shunters' board and handrails feature nicely in this image which was captured on Saturday 7th October 1950. Note the black paint has been applied around the number 69154; those figures were put on during the week ending 3rd June 1948 when the N15 was undergoing a Heavy Intermediate overhaul, again at Cowlairs works. The 4MTT above the number is new as is the RA6 and of course that lining. Dunfermline had nine of these engines at the time this photograph was recorded, down just one on the ten handed over at Nationalisation. At Grouping this engine was resident here as NBR No.917 along with sisters Nos.389, 390, and 918. Thirty more of the class were delivered during the LNER era and Dunfermline was one of the sheds to benefit from this addition and by midnight on 31st December 1927 three more N15 had joined the original quartet – Nos.9147, 9524, and 9527. *K.H. Cockerill (ARPT)*.

It is September 1955 and Y9 No.68101 with its four-wheel wooden-bodied tender, was working as station pilot at Dunfermline Upper. This diminutive but extremely useful tank engine had been allocated to Dunfermline since transferring from Kipps on 4th August 1932. It was to work from 62C until condemned on 8th October 1962 and then be taken to Inverurie where it was broken up in January 1963. However, before then a visit to the locomotive works at Cowlairs during the summer of 1956 would see the four-coupled engine receiving a General overhaul which would set it up for a good few years pottering about Dunfermline and district. Note the footplateman with collar and tie, and those highly polished shoes! One can see the need for overalls, and those gloves, even in summer. Also, see V3 67675 lurking in the background. *C.J.B. Sanderson (ARPT)*.

Thursday 14th May 1959, rear yard of Dunfermline shed. Y9 No.68101 was the only one of her class working from Dunfermline during BR times. Even before Grouping Dunfermline had housed a Y9 with No.40 (9040 from 14th November 1925) being resident until relieved by 10088 (8101 from 1st September 1946) in August 1932 so that No.9040 could attend Cowlairs works for a General overhaul. This rear three-quarter view enables us to discern some of the cab details on the Y9 including being able to see why those tenders were necessary. Note the drop down canvas cover giving minimal protection from the weather. The method of getting coal from the tender to the footplate or directly into the firebox would give H&S inspectors nightmares today but such is progress we no longer have to resort to making a living in such a haphazard way. *I.W. Coulson (ARPT).*

This siding on the south side of the shed yard was formerly used to stack coal – note the redundant sleepers in the foreground – but on 3rd June 1952 when this image was recorded, coal was rather short and BR had used much of its ground stocks during the period 1948 to 1951 when the whole country felt the effects of the coal shortage. Besides cancelling certain services and curtailing others, BR decided to convert hundreds of steam locomotives to burn oil. The conversion and the required infrastructure for storing, processing and delivering the oil was costly but the whole exercise became meaningless after the oil also became short in supply. The coal mines gradually came back up to projected levels of supply but nevertheless most of the coal stacks were never to appear again. The locomotive interest here is C15 No.67453 one of three Atlantic tanks allocated to Dunfermline at the time. Arriving at Dunfermline on 25th November 1932 after a four year residency at Dundee, the C15 never left 62C until condemned on 28th January 1954. She was destined never to carry the BR emblem and had to make do with that faded LNER lettering until scrapped. *C.J.B. Sanderson (ARPT).*

This view of the north side of the shed yard on 5th April 1953 reveals the fairly new ash bunker which was constructed of concrete and was a useful addition to the servicing procedure at 62C. Gresley K2 No.61721 was another addition to the Dunfermline allocation but could not be described as new – or even clean – as it takes up position alongside a WD 2-8-0 and one of the visiting WD 2-10-0s, both unidentified. No.61721 started life as a K1 in February 1913 and was rebuilt to K2 standard during a five month sojourn in Doncaster works which ended 19th March 1921. 62C had three of these useful 2-6-0s allocated from 1952 – 61721, 61758, and 61770 – and they served the shed until the late Fifties when they were condemned. No.61721 was a latecomer to Scotland, as were all three of the Dunfermline trio, and transferred from Stratford to Eastfield on 3rd June 1951. It moved over to Fife on 20th January 1952. Including its two Scottish depots, this K2 transferred no less than fifteen times during its forty-six year life. After being condemned on the penultimate day of 1959, it was sold to a private scrap yard three months later. *F.W. Hampson (ARPT)*.

The locomotive in this 3rd June 1952 photograph is K2 No.61721 again – minus a front number plate – but the real subject of this image is the panel of the breakdown train riding van on the right. The legend on the panel states: RIDER & TOOL VAN LOCOMOTIVE DEPT. DUNFERMLINE BURNTISLAND DIST. 971513. The panel above states L N E R which essentially dates the vehicle or rather the legend on the panel which when it was sign-written at the start of the LNER, Burntisland was the head shed for the district! *C.J.B. Sanderson (ARPT)*.

The shed roof was renewed during 1955 using prefabricated concrete units which did not require any bolts or fixings as they simply slotted within each other. Supported on five concrete columns – which replaced some twenty-seven cast-iron columns – the 'new' roof was stated to weigh some 520 tons! Here is the 'new' roof ten years later on Saturday 1st May 1965 with the glazing units still allowing plenty of natural light into what was normally a quite dismay atmosphere. Two stalwart 0-6-0s represent some of the steam allocation on this date – J37 64599 and J38 65921 – whilst diesel shunters have already come home for the weekend! Dunfermline had a number of these shunters with the first lot – North British Locomotive Co. 0-4-0 DHs – arriving during 1957/58. Both 200 h.p. and 225 h.p. diesel-hydraulic versions were allocated with D2704 being the second NBL diesel to arrive – on 22nd February 1958 – after 11707 on 2nd November 1957. They then became a regular feature as D2716, 11717, 11718, D2743 and D2644 all became residents. The latter pair actually spent more time at Alloa as they were sub-shedded there virtually after arrival at 62C on 18th and 27th April 1959 respectively. In April 1966 three Barclay 0-4-0 204 h.p. diesel mechanical shunters arrived – D2413, D2416, and D2417 – but they re-allocated to Leith Central in May 1967. To take their place and to replace some of the NBL shunters withdrawn in 1967, three Hunslet 0-6-0 204 h.p. diesel-mechanical shunters arrived from June 1967 with a fourth example transferring in on 2nd December 1967. By 30th December 1967 all four were withdrawn and the remaining diesel shunters had been transferred away during the interim. Dunfermline was now bereft of diesel motive power; steam had gone during the previous May. Finally on the diesel front one of the ex-LMS 0-6-0 350 h.p. diesel-electric shunters, No.12107 arrived from Thornton on 17th June 1967 but it too – one of the more reliable shunting types – was withdrawn on that penultimate day of 1967. *N.W. Skinner (ARPT).*

J38 No.65933 had been a part of the Dunfermline allocation since 5th June 1928 but on 1st May 1965 it was laid-up and stored awaiting sale for scrap after being condemned on the previous 17th April. The floodlights belonging to the football stadium known as East End Park, home to Dunfermline Athletic F.C., can be seen in the background. That football club thrives in 2020 but all traces of Dunfermline's steam locomotive shed have gone. *N.W. Skinner (ARPT).*

J37 No.64568, an example of the ultimate North British Railway 0-6-0 outside the shed in June 1956. Some one hundred and four of these locomotives were built between 1914 and 1921, the bulk constructed at the Atlas works of the NB Loco. Co. (69) whilst Cowlairs works turned out thirty-five. Initially Dunfermline has just three of them – 467, 469, and 488 – but shortly after Grouping that number became just two as the Gresley J38 started to arrive so that by 1927 ten of the LNER 0-6-0s were resident. However, by Nationalisation the tables were set mainly in favour of the J37s with fourteen in residence against thirteen J38. All of the ancient 0-6-0s of classes J31, J33 and J34 had gone. A decent example of Class J38 – No.65928 – languishes in the background. That particular J38 came to Dunfermline on 12th December 1943 from Dundee. It remained allocated to the end and was condemned on 28th December 1962 having been placed into store during the previous 4th September. *C.J.B. Sanderson (ARPT)*.

The western end of the engine shed at midday on Saturday 6th June 1959 with J35 No.64476 and J37 No.64597 – both residents – serviced and ready for Monday's tasks. The allocation here was in decline compared with the seventy-odd locomotives allocated when BR came into being. The J35s remained constant at ten examples whereas J37 class had lost a third to just eight engines at 62C. The WD 2-8-0 population was slowly receding from a dozen to nine. At Grouping Dunfermline had thirty-one 0-6-0 tender engines – spread over six classes – from a total allocation of fifty-one locomotives. *C.J.B. Sanderson (ARPT).*

A little gathering at the side of the shed on that Saturday in June 1959 with J88 No.68346 hogging centre stage; N15 No.69202 is behind. *C.J.B. Sanderson (ARPT).*

BR Standard Cl.4 No.76110 was one of the Thornton 'trio' which transferred to Dunfermline in 1960. This view taken during the summer of 1962 – 26th July – reveals the engines were not being cleaned but at least they were being maintained! *C.J.B. Sanderson (ARPT).*

WD 2-8-0 No.90553 laid-up on Thursday 26th July 1962. Being chiefly engaged in moving coal from the local collieries, Dunfermline shed had to work around the summer holiday periods being taken by the miners. Whole pits would close for a fortnight and production fell to zero with only maintenance was carried out beneath ground. Seasonal demand for coal would also fall during the summer months and so Dunfermline and other depots in similar situations would temporarily store their heavy freight locomotives. Note the extremely tidy yard! *C.J.B. Sanderson (ARPT)*.

Two of Dunfermline's residents – B1 No.61072 and WD No.90386 – peer out of the west end of the shed on Sunday 19th June 1966. *A. Ives (ARPT).*

J38 No.65917 stabled at the west end of the shed 19th June 1966. Exactly five months away from withdrawal, the 0-6-0 was about to end its operational life where it all began in March 1926. *A. Ives (ARPT).*

C15 No.67469 was one of Dunfermline's trio of Atlantic tanks – 67453 and 67466 were the others – and in July 1950 this example was somewhere between being clean or dirty; it seems that the latter condition is winning but perhaps the shed's cleaners will put in an appearance and put the shine back onto the 2PT. Considering the engine had only just returned from its final General overhaul and repaint at Cowlairs in May, the standards at 62C were slipping somewhat. As a sort of twist on a locomotives' daily routine, this C15 was transferred to the M&EE Burntisland workshop for stationary boiler duties from 13th July to 3rd August 1950, and again from 12th to 26th July 1951, and yet again from 9th to 20th July 1952. From this angle it is easy to see the continuation of the side tank and wheel splasher, the former taking up so much space within the cab. *C.J.B. Sanderson (ARPT).*

Still sporting its former owners' marks and numbers, J88 No.8345 was stabled alongside Dunfermline shed in July 1950. 62C had three of these little 0-6-0Ts in 1950 – 68346 and 68351(both recent acquisitions from Stirling) being the other two – and their main job it appears was working from Alloa sub shed, from where two of them performed at the nearby docks whilst the third was held in reserve at Dunfermline. It's a shame today's railways don't have such assets in reserve but it's all about profit now rather than service! The 0-6-0T eventually lost its LNER livery when it visited Cowlairs shops for a General overhaul – 13th to 30th June 1951 – and came out as 68345. Arriving at Dunfermline on 20th February 1949 from Eastfield, the J88 moved back to 65A at the end of August 1958 as diesel shunters took over what was left of their docks duties. By 1960 the docks themselves were finished with coal exports virtually nil and the larger sea-going vessels unable to navigate the upper reaches of the river. No.68345 was condemned at Kipps shed on 28th December 1962 just as the extreme cold set in! *C.J.B. Sanderson (ARPT).*

ALLOA

Alloa Sunday 27th June 1948. Sub to Dunfermline, this shed was opened in 1885 by the North British Railway and was located just east of Alloa station on the north side of the Dunfermline line. During BR days – and I presume in the LNER period too – the shed was in the charge of a Fitter, and there were twenty-one sets of footplate men all of whom except the Dock Pilot crews rotated round the Alva branch passenger turns, main line goods to Cadder and Inverkeithing, pick-up goods, Kincardine, local coal trains from Devon sidings, and the station goods pilot. A C15 shared the Alva passenger job with a J36, and J37s worked the main line goods and some local jobs were also done by J36s. A J36 was used as station pilot and J88s performed the Dock Pilots. In February 1952 the shed housed two J35, three J36, two J88, and a C15. Another visit on Saturday 6th June 1953 found the following stabled: J35 Nos.64487, 64525, J36 Nos.65281, 65307, 65320, J88 Nos.68345, 68346, and C15 No.67469. The C15 worked the Alva branch but on Monday 5th October 1953 it was reported that J36 No.65307 was employed. A year later, on Saturday 18th September 1954 the following engines were on shed: C15 No.67466, J35 No.64493, J36 Nos.65281, 65307, 65320, J37 Nos.64574, 64630, and J88 Nos.68345, 68351. *K.H. Cockerill (ARPT)*.

An undated view of the shed on a summer's afternoon, with J38 No.65903 joining the ever changing allocation; to the right is WD 2-8-0 No.90229 which arrived at Dunfermline from Polmadie on 15th June 1963 so giving us an idea of the date. Both locomotives were condemned in 1966 so we have a basic three year period to look at but May 1965 seems a reasonable date. A considerable amount of coal traffic passed through Alloa, and British Railways announced in September 1954 a plan to create a new 15-siding marshalling yard at Alloa at an estimated cost of £500,000. The resultant Alloa new yard was brought into full operation at the end of May 1957 with a 350 h.p. 0-6-0 diesel-electric shunting locomotive 13211 in residence (the DE shunter had been delivered new to Thornton on 24th February 1956 but it was transferred to Eastfield a month before the new Alloa yard became fully operational so it looks as though 62A kept hold of the diesel a tad longer than necessary). The opening of the yard reduced the duties of the shed at Stirling Shore Road and three of their J37s were transferred to Dundee. *Maurice Burns*.

The three and a half mile Alva branch closed from 1st November 1954. The last train – 1303 ex-Alloa (departed 1308 awaiting a connection from Glasgow), returned from Alva at 1333 – ran on Saturday 30th October hauled by C15 No.67466 with two well-filled coaches. No.65307 had made a few runs earlier in the day. The complement of locomotives working from Alloa was reduced to eight after the withdrawal of the Alva branch passenger services; the C15 no longer required. On New Year's Day 1955 the allocation was: J35 No.64505, J36 Nos.65253, 65281, 65323, J37 Nos.64561, 64574, J88 Nos.68346, 68351. This view of the shed from summer 1955 shows the aforementioned J36 and J37 No.64567. The grounded coach body was one of two which comprised the staff amenities and office. *K.H. Cockerill (ARPT).*

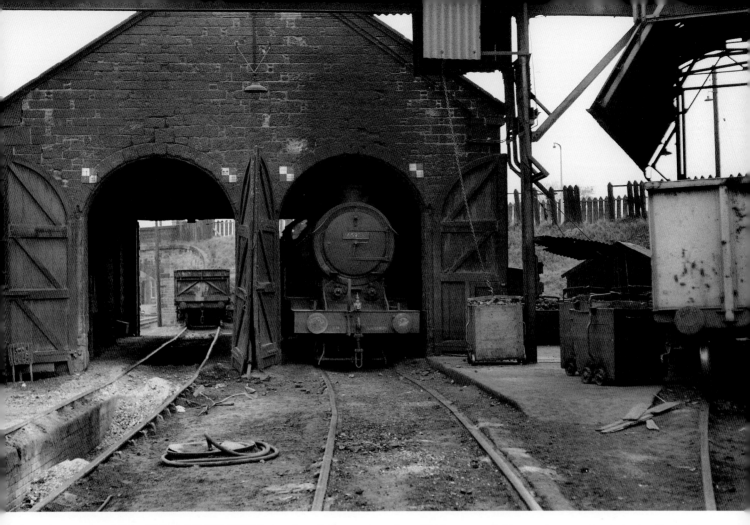

Saturday morning, 1st May 1965 with J38 No.65906 being the only locomotive at home! This un-crowded image gives us a chance to view the coaling facility which was quite a rare beast on BR, if not unique in its plan form, and was simple in execution whereby a motorised lifting mechanism ran along – hung from – a girder (a bit like a telpher unit in a gasworks for instance) and was able to lift pre-filled, four-wheeled buckets which had been loaded from the wagons under the cover of the shelter. Once hauled aloft the buckets were positioned above the tender bunker where a lever was operated which allowed the bucket to upend itself and thereby empty its contents into the tender. Note that the control box on the column has also got a shelter although that looks a bit Heath Robinson rather than part of the original package. The allocation appeared to be fairly consistent through the early BR period with virtually the same locomotives serving this sub-shed for long periods. They were changed when repairs were required. On 13th November 1956 the following were in residence: 64475, 64487, 64493, 64556, 64567, 64604, 65281, 65320, 68345, and 68351. By that date one of the J88s worked the Alloa goods and the traffic on the Harbour branch whilst the other was spare. Looking at the doors on the shed, it would be a safe bet to state that they had probably never been closed from the day the shed opened. *N.W. Skinner (ARPT)*.

The western end of the shed on 19th June 1966 with Dunfermline J38 No.65918, and Thornton Junction based B1 No.61132 spending the weekend at the shed. A new gable end was constructed of common brick with a rolled steel joist spanning the two stabling roads. Why the change in gable is unknown; speculatively perhaps a locomotive was a bit slow in applying its brakes and collided with the original dead-end structure? The change did allow the greater clearance for personnel compared with the front, east end arches. A little known fact but one that all shed aficionados should know is that Alloa was the only engine shed in Clackmannanshire during BR days, and except for the tiny one-road shed at Alva to the north, which closed in 1931, was the only engine shed in the county. The Caledonian had a one-road shed in Alloa which opened in 1903 but that too closed in 1930 so doesn't really count. back to our image, it will be noticed that diesel locomotives are present on this date and Dunfermline used to supply a couple of the NBL 0-4-0DH to Alloa from about summer 1959 onwards however by 1966 the little diesels were out of favour D2743 having already been transferred to Crewe works in 1965. The cab in the picture here would be that of D2744 which moved on to St Margarets in July 1966. *A. Ives (ARPT)*.

Alloa on Sunday 19th June 1966. Towards the end of steam the pre and post Grouping designs were being scrapped at an alarming rate and LNER Standard and BR Standard types were seen more often doing the work. Centre stage is Dundee B1 No.61340 which transferred to Dunfermline on 26th August next but moved back to 62B on 13th November. Buffered-up is BR Standard Cl.4 No.76110 the fortunes of which we have followed from Thornton to Dunfermline and now having a stint at the Alloa sub-shed. *A. Ives (ARPT).*

Alloa shed on Friday 2nd October 1959 with a pair of 0-6-0s – J37 No.64617 identified – simmering in the evening sun. Besides Alloa, other sub sheds located in the Dunfermline district were: Loch Leven which closed in 1951; Inverkeithing – a signing-on point. However, four engines were stationed all week there for banking and pilot duties, returning to Dunfermline at weekends. During the week ending 12th November 1956 the following were in use: J35 Nos.64480, 64496, 64505, N15 No.69164. Those used for banking had slip couplings at both ends; Kelty – another signing-on point. Four N15s were stationed here for pilot work. Leaving Dunfermline on Monday mornings they would stay away until the following weekend whence they returned. *W.S. Sellar*.